Walk Forward:

Navigating the Job Loss Journey with Truth, Triumph, and Tools

Walk Forward: Navigating The Job Loss Journey With Truth, Triumph, And Tools

Juanita Moore & Nichole Thompson

 Printed in the United States of America.
Book design by Juanita Moore & Nichole Thompson
Cover design by Nichole Thompson
ISBN - Paperback: 9798904171841
First Edition: April 2026

Dedication

Dedication from Juanita Moore:

I dedicate this book to the loving memory of my parents, Mr. Eddie W. Moore and Mrs. Eloise Moore–powerhouses of faith who spent their lives encouraging others, spreading joy, and caring for everyone around them. Their power in laughter, and ongoing supportive words "baby, keep going on" gave me the ability to walk forward with confidence, to trust my heavenly Father always and a desire to serve others.

Dedication from Nichole T. Thompson:

To my Heavenly Father, who has never forgotten me. Through this experience, I have come to know more deeply that You never will (Isaiah 49:15–16).

To my family, who walked beside me through this season. Even in the uncertainty, I will always treasure the quiet conversations with my mother at her bedside and the mid-afternoon bike rides along the Detroit River with my baby girls.

Table of Contents

Introduction

If you are holding this book, something in your professional life or someone you care about has shifted. It may have ended without warning. You may have sensed over time that something was changing long before the official conversation happened. It may have arrived when you were already carrying a lot in other areas of your life. However it happened, the disruption is real, and you are not alone.

Let's agree that losing a job changes more than income. It changes how you see yourself. This book was written for several kinds of readers. It is for the employee who feels disoriented after job loss, waking up to mornings that feel unfamiliar. It is for the seasoned professional who wants to rebuild with clarity instead of panic. It is for the corporate leader or HR professional seeking to better understand the often unspoken human impact behind these decisions. It is for the person of faith wrestling with questions of identity and purpose, and for the reader who may not share that faith but still desires steadiness, practical wisdom, and a way forward.

We did not write this book from theory. We wrote it from lived experience. We wrote it from our own job losses layered with financial responsibility, caregiving, expectations, and private grief. We wrote it from honest conversations that were sometimes raw and often unfinished. We wrote it from the quiet courage required to keep showing up when the plan you trusted no longer existed.

There is another reason this book exists. Language matters. When we talk about layoffs or job loss, the words can quickly become abstract. The words turn into strategy, restructuring, or market shifts. Over time, the human being at the center of the experience disappears. The impact becomes data. The story becomes a process. The person unintentionally becomes a line item.

Recent data shows how large the impact truly is. In 2025 alone, roughly 21 million layoffs and discharges were recorded in the United States, but that number represents far more than labor statistics.

It represents millions of individuals—parents, spouses, caregivers, and neighbors—each with responsibilities that do not pause when employment does.

Behind every separation is a household adjusting to uncertainty, recalculating budgets, and carrying the emotional weight of instability.

Layoffs are not just numbers. They are lives. This book intentionally addresses the employee's concerns and helps them navigate the language of layoffs.

Too often we hear that a company will "lay off ten percent" or "reduce headcount." The words sound procedural, almost distant, almost like they are not even about people.

But those decisions are not abstract. They are actual employee layoffs—real people whose livelihoods are interrupted, and whose families must adjust to uncertainty.

Behind every restructuring is a household recalculating their stability.

eeec3eed3It is our intention throughout this book that when we talk about layoffs, we are always talking about people and the families impacted. Not to assign blame, but to keep the human reality clearly in view as we talk about what it takes to move forward.

Our purpose is simple, even if the journey is not.

Many people quietly question their own reactions during seasons like this. They wonder why the disruption lingers longer than expected or why it feels harder to move forward than they imagined. If that has been your experience, you are not alone. We felt many of those same tensions ourselves.

We want to create space for honesty and strategy, for grief, and forward movement.

Loss may change your path, but it does not erase your worth.

As you move through this book, our hope is that you begin to feel a little more steady as you deal with the very real weight of job loss, the disruption to your identity, and the day to day uncertainty this season can bring. That you start to regain some clarity and confidence as you wrestle with questions about your future, your value, and what comes next.

We can't promise how your situation will unfold, but we can show you, because we have lived it, that there is another side to this experience.

We have each moved forward in different ways. One of us returned to employment, and the other stepped into building a small business. Neither path was immediate, and neither came without challenge, but both required us to face this season courageously and keep going.

Throughout the book, and within the appendices, you will also find practical information, guidance, and encouragement to support you in the real, everyday decisions this season requires.

This book is divided into three sections addressing different phases of your job loss journey: **Truth**, **Triumph**, and **Tools**.

Truth

Chapter 1
The Day

For many people, there are moments in time that reshape your professional life without asking your permission. The DAY is one of those moments in life that quietly divides time into two halves: before and after. It likely began as an ordinary day. A calendar notification appeared. A meeting request slid into your inbox. Nothing about it seemed unusual. Meetings, of course, happen every day. Conversations are routine. You may have continued working, unaware that within minutes your sense of stability would shift.

Then Human Resources joined the call...

In that instant, something inside you dropped. Your body understood before your mind did. There is a split second between knowing and hearing—a suspended pause where confusion, disbelief, fear, and grief rush forward all at once. The words themselves may blur, but their meaning does not: you are being let go.

Sometimes the language is softened. They say "restructure." They say "realignment." They say "reduction." The terms are polished and careful. But none of them feel true in that moment. What you feel is loss.

Time slows. You hear the explanation, but your thoughts race ahead. What do you tell your family? How will the mortgage be paid? What about paying for tuition, insurance, and the obligations waiting quietly on the kitchen counter? What happens tomorrow morning when the alarm goes off and there is nowhere you are required to be?

Then, you are asked to turn in your badge.

You are asked to clear your laptop. You are asked to watch your access disappear in real time.

Yesterday you belonged. Today, you do not.

Work is not only income. It is structure. It is rhythm. It is connection. It is a way of introducing yourself. When it ends abruptly, the absence is loud.

Perhaps there were warning signs. Perhaps there were none. When the screen went dark and the corporate call ended, you may have remained seated, staring at nothing in particular. It was not simply a job that concluded. It felt like a version of you had been dismissed along with it.

If you are in this space right now, pause.

This day has taken enough from you. Today is not for solving every problem or mapping out the next five years. Today is for steadying yourself. Call one trusted person. Eat something, even if you have no appetite. Rest, even if sleep feels distant. Delay major decisions.

The Day may have shaken you, but it did not erase your capability. It did not cancel your experience. It did not revoke your identity. What ended was a role—a title—a place within an organizational chart. What remains is your skill, your character, and the professional story that still belongs to you.

This is the beginning of a new chapter, even if you did not choose it. And while the beginning feels uncertain, it is still a beginning.

*"What ended was a role -
not your skill,
not your character, and
not the professional story
that still belongs to you."*

Chapter 2
What Do I Tell My Family?

When the meeting ends, and the first wave of shock begins to settle, there is another question that rises quietly: What do I tell my family?

The silence after the news can feel heavier than the news itself. It is no longer just about you. It is about the people whose lives are tied to yours, the ones who depend on the rhythm your work provided.

For many people, family is not only who you love. It is who you provide for. The mortgage payment that withdraws each month without thought.

Tuition deadlines.
Car notes.
Insurance.
Retirement contributions.
Groceries that appear on the table because your paycheck made them possible.

Work was more than income. It was structure. Stability. A quiet promise that things were handled.

When that structure shifts, it can feel as if everyone standing beneath it is suddenly exposed.

In that space, shame often slips in.

It does not shout. It whispers.

They will see me differently.
I should have prevented this. I failed.

Your mind starts rewriting the story as if this outcome were entirely yours to carry.

But shame rarely tells the whole truth.

Job loss is more than structural. It is financial. It is strategic. It may be tied to decisions made far above you or far away from your performance, yet because family is personal, the impact feels personal. When your role includes provision, it can be hard to separate circumstance from self-worth.

There is often what many quietly call the "driveway moment". You sit in the car longer than usual with your hands resting on the steering wheel, rehearsing what you will say. You search for the right tone. The right words. The right way to soften the news. You measure how much of your fear to show.

You may even consider pretending for a few days—you would get dressed, leave the house, keep up appearances just to delay the conversation. Avoidance can feel protective. But pretending only adds pressure. It leaves you alone at the very moment you need support.

Lead with honesty, even imperfect honesty, will feel steadier over time.

The first conversation does not need to be polished. It needs to be real.

With a spouse or partner, it may sound like, "Today I was let go. I'm still processing it, but I want us to face this together."

With children, it may be, "My job ended today. That might change some things, but it doesn't change how much I love you or how committed I am to our family."

With a close friend, perhaps, "I was part of a layoff. I'm taking this one step at a time."

The words do not have to be extraordinary. They simply need to be true.

You do not need to perform strength. You need to show resilience. There is a difference. Performed strength hides fear and rushes to solutions. Resilience acknowledges something happened and keeps moving anyway.

Your family does not need you to be perfect. They need you to be present.

Not everyone will respond the way you hope. Some may rush to fix it. Some may minimize your feelings. Some may not know what to say. Their reactions reflect their own discomfort, not your value.

Shame loses power when it is spoken aloud. It grows in silence. However, it weakens when shared.

You are not less capable because your job ended. You are not less faithful. You are not less worthy. You are navigating change and that is not the same as failure.

Speak your story without shrinking yourself in the process. The conversation may be difficult, but difficulty does not define you. It reveals your courage to stand in truth, even when the outcome was not what you chose.

"Your family does not need you to be perfect. They need you to be present."

Chapter 3
The Morning After

Morning comes whether you feel ready or not.

For a brief second, everything feels normal. The room is quiet. The light filters in like it always has. Then memory returns. The meeting. The words. The ending. It settles in again, and the weight presses against the start of a new day.

You may reach for your phone out of habit. Or glance at your calendar. No meetings. No reminders. No familiar rhythm guiding you forward.

Yesterday your day had structure.
Today there is silence.

And that silence can feel loud.

Without the distraction of work, your mind begins to spin.

What now?
How long will this last?
What if I don't recover quickly?
What if this becomes something bigger than I can manage?

The questions stack on top of one another until it feels hard to breathe.

This is where compounded loss begins to surface. It is rarely just about a job. It touches responsibility. Identity. Security. It may stir up older grief that never fully settled. Job loss does not land in an empty space. It collides with everything already in motion.

Bills still arrive.
The family still needs you.
Plans that once felt steady now feel fragile.

When your thoughts are racing in every direction, resist the urge to fix everything at once.

You do not rebuild your career on the first morning.
You steady yourself.

Start small.
Take a slow breath.
Choose good nutrition for much needed fuel.
Call one trusted person.
Step outside for a few minutes and move your body.
Choose one task. Not ten. One.
Open one email.

Look at one document.
Take one step.

There may be practical and financial details waiting for you. Messages about final pay, benefits, or next steps may still be sitting in your inbox or spread across your table. For some, there may be severance to review. For others, there may be immediate concerns about income and support. Forms related to unemployment or assistance may feel like too much to face right now, and that is understandable.

You do not have to figure all of that out alone.

We will walk through these steps in a later chapter and in the appendices of this book. We have gathered practical resources to support you, including unemployment information for all fifty states, mental health support, and public health and income assistance programs. Those resources will be there when you are ready.

You do not have to complete everything today.

But you do have to begin.

Stability returns in layers. First, your breathing steadies. Then your thinking clears. Then you face the numbers. Then you make a plan.

Panic may push you to act quickly, but it rarely gives you clarity.

You are not weak because this feels heavy. You are adjusting to impact. That takes time.

The swirl in your mind will not last forever. But clarity will require your participation. It asks you to slow down long enough to think. To choose one wise step instead of ten frantic ones.

You do not have to solve your entire future today.

You only have to take the next step.
And then, when you are ready, the one after that.

And then you keep walking forward.

"You do not rebuild your career on the first morning - you steady yourself."

Chapter 4
What's Given And What You Need

At some point, after the first waves of shock fade the next steps begin to surface.

For some, that may come in the form of a list of to-do items provided, including final exit documents to review, financial forms to sign off on, forms to complete, with important deadlines to meet. For others, it may be far less formal. A brief conversation or a short email with limited direction on what comes next.

However it shows up, you are left with information to process and decisions to make.

So begin there.

Take care of what needs to be done.
Review what has been provided.
Pay attention to deadlines. .
Complete what is required of you.

There are a few things that matter right away.

✔Be aware of any deadlines tied to your separation.
✔Understand when your benefits change and what options may be available to you.
✔Confirm your final compensation details.
✔Secure copies of important employment records while you still have access.

Also, take a moment to look ahead.

✔Make sure you know how you will receive your W-2 for the following year and that your contact information is up to date.
✔Understand what happens to your retirement account, including whether it remains in place, needs to be rolled over, or requires a decision within a certain timeframe.

Handle these step by step. This is not about doing everything at once. It is about making sure you are protected while everything still feels unsettled.

And even after you have done all of that, you may still find yourself sitting with a quiet but persistent thought.

Something still feels missing.

This is the gap, the space between what was provided and what you actually needed in that moment.

The information may have been complete.
The exit process may have been handled carefully and correctly.

But you were not just processing paperwork.
You were processing loss.

What has been significant for you is reduced to next steps, and no document can fully account for that.

Ideally it may have felt different if there had been more space for the human side of the experience.

A moment to acknowledge what just happened and how it may compound with other things.
A conversation that felt less procedural and more personal.
A sense that someone recognized not just the role you held, but the contribution you made.
A pause that allowed the moment to land before moving straight into action.

These things are not often part of this process, but their absence can be felt.

That is the gap.

Recognizing the gap does not change what happened, but it does help *you* understand your own response to it.

You are not struggling because you missed something.

You are responding to something that was never fully addressed in the time humans need.

So as you move forward, give yourself permission to take care of both sides of this experience.

Take care of your responsibilities, but do not ignore yourself in the process.

Pause when you need to.
Stay connected to people who see you beyond your role.

You do not have to rush to make everything feel resolved.

What was removed was a position.

What remains is a capable, experienced person, still able to contribute, still able to rebuild, and still able to move forward.

"What was removed was a position. What remains is a capable, experienced, and value person."

Chapter 5
Survival Mode

Today, survival mode begins.

The tenderness of the first shock begins to fade and more focus begins to take over.

When you carry responsibility, children who depend on you, bills that do not pause, aging parents who still look to you for steadiness, and even your individual obligations, there is no time for staying down for long.

You wake up.

You wash your face.

You look in the mirror and say, "Let's go again."

Survival mode is not weakness. It is instinct. It is the body and mind shifting toward protection and provision.

Almost immediately, your thoughts turn practical. You review the numbers. You tighten the budget. You scan the calendar. Applications are sent. Phone calls are made.

You move certainly not because you feel strong, but because movement is required.

You feel torn as you move.

Your faith or outlook may whisper provision while fear shouts uncertainty. Both can exist at the same time.

You might pray for open doors while refreshing your inbox. You might speak hope out loud while privately calculating how long savings will stretch.

That tension does not mean you are unstable. It means you are human.

Rejection emails arrive. Silence stretches longer than you hoped. You begin to question timing. You wonder why progress feels slower than you expected.

Still, you continue.

Another résumé update.

Another tailored cover letter.

Another conversation.

That steady repetition matters more than it feels like at the moment.

Survival is practical work. It is both spreadsheets and prayer sitting on the same table. It is calling creditors for information and calling friends for encouragement. It is staying engaged when motivation dips and fatigue creeps in. There is dignity in that persistence.

In more practical terms, remember you should prioritize and protect what matters most first. Take care of housing and food before appearance. Insurance should come before impulse decisions. Essentials before extras or upgrades.

These choices sound obvious for some but can get cloudy in difficult times. .

If possible, communicate early with lenders. File for unemployment promptly. Understand your severance timeline. Track expenses so the numbers are visible instead of imagined.

Fear grows more when things are vague and clarity settles the mind.

Emotionally, create some rhythm. Wake up at a consistent time. Move your body.

Limit job searching to focused blocks so it does not consume every hour. Rest without guilt. Even in survival mode, you are not meant to run at crisis speed forever.

Survival mode is temporary, but it is necessary. It reveals what matters. It strips away what does not. It builds endurance quietly, day by day.

You are not failing. You are enduring.

And endurance, sustained over time, becomes strength.

Pause and remind yourself: you are stabilizing what matters most.

That is wisdom in motion.

"Survival mode is not weakness. It is instinct."

Chapter 6
Hello, My Name is...

You scroll through job listings, and something feels off.

On paper, you qualify for the job. You have the experience. You understand the work. You could do many of these jobs well.

And still, something doesn't sit right.

It's hard to explain. But you feel it.

After loss, a question returns—one you may not have asked in years:

What do I even want now?

Not what is available.
Not what looks impressive.
Not what pays the most.

What actually fits?

Before that question can be answered, something else often surfaces.

It happens over time, the work can quietly blend into personal identity. Job titles carry responsibility and buy calendars reflect importance. Without even realizing it, many professionals begin to measure their self worth by how busy they are and how much they produce. Therefore when that structure disappears, something deeper is uncovered and unsettled.

The question is no longer only about work. It becomes more personal:

Who am I now?

You may have worn many titles over the years. Manager. Director. Specialist. Provider. Expert. Everyone of these individual roles required skill and carried responsibility. Over time, the work itself became part of how you introduced yourself, how you measured progress, how you understood your value in organizations, community and the world.

So when the roles end, the disruption reaches deeper than you could have ever imagined.

Now new introductions feel awkward. Confidence wavers. The absence of that title or role is not only financial . It is personal. It is your shaken identity.

However there is something steady beneath all of that. **You Are**. The special skills, knowledge and abilities you hold that allowed you to earn and carry those titles still remain.

This season invites you to rebuild from deeper inside.

Instead of asking, "What do I do?" begin asking, "Who am I?"

A few things to remember...

Skills can be applied in different settings. Character travels into every room.

You are not starting over from nothing. You are returning to the foundation.

When identity begins to settle, the question about work becomes easier to approach.

Instead of asking only, *What job can I get?* try asking a better question, ***Where will I grow well?***

Look for patterns.

When have you felt most engaged?

What problems do you enjoy solving?

What kind of environment helps you think clearly?

A Moment for Reflection (Activity)

Take a few minutes to think about who you are beyond a job title.

Try writing a few statements that begin with "I am".

Let them describe your character rather than your position.

I am dependable.

I am thoughtful.

I am disciplined.

I am creative.

I am steady under pressure.

I am resilient.

Notice the difference.

These statements are not tied to earnings. They do not require a title. They travel with you.

When did you feel proud of your work—not just paid for it?

These questions are not selfish. They are clarifying.

Some people will return to similar roles with more confidence. Some will change industries.

Some will build something of their own. Others may take temporary roles while they plan the next step.

There is no single right answer.

What matters is that you are choosing with awareness rather than reacting to urgency. For some, that awareness comes through quiet reflection, prayer, or meditation as you seek clarity for what comes next.

"Skills can be applied in different settings. Character travels into every room."

Triumph

Chapter 7
Showing Up Again
Rebuilding Your Network Without Your Title

In today's job market, submitting applications and waiting is rarely enough.

Positions are posted. Portals exist. However, hiring decisions often move through familiarity and trust—through someone saying, *"I know that person. They are solid."*

Comfort still carries weight.

Research shows that many roles are filled through relationships, referrals, or internal connections rather than open applications. In fact, more than half of workers report landing a job through someone they knew (LinkedIn, 2016). It may not always feel fair, but it reflects how hiring often works in practice.

Relationships matter.

During one professional transition, one of us reached out to a respected and highly visible HR Leader for perspective. The goal was not sympathy. The goal was information and clarity.

He paused and said something that stayed with us:

“The game has changed. Networking matters. People need to feel comfortable endorsing you.”

That word stayed with us.

Comfortable.

After admitting that the professional network felt thin, the needed response was equally clear.

“You need to reintroduce yourself.”

Not quietly.

Not wait for when confidence fully returned.

NOW!

Several professional gatherings were suggested across the state including conferences, leadership forums, and industry events. Some felt intimidating. Some of them required travel. Others simply required courage. Some required money.

The decision was simple.

Register. Show up.

From late spring through the end of the year, showing up became consistent.

Some events offered transition pricing.

Additionally, some volunteer opportunities appeared unexpectedly.

Some required sacrifice.

But something important began to form.

Familiar faces.

Repeated conversations.

Trust built slowly instead of instantly.

Did attending immediately produce a job offer?

No.

But something stronger was developing.

Visibility.

Relationships.

Credibility built through presence.

That is the long game of networking.

Not urgency.

Not performance.

Presence.

Learning how to introduce yourself without performing is a super power.

Re-entering professional spaces after job loss can feel exposing.

There is no title reinforcing identity. No company logo adding weight to introductions.

No organizational chart placing your name neatly within a structure.

It is natural to wonder how to enter the room.

One shift proved surprisingly powerful: stop performing.

Instead of rehearsing a polished biography, introductions became simple.

Name.

Professional lane.

Reason for being there.

Then listen.

You are no longer performing. You are participating.

You still have something to offer the room.

When the focus moves from "How do I impress?" to "How do I connect?", the energy changes. Networking stops feeling like an audition and starts feeling like alignment.

Sometimes the bravest act is simply staying in the room.

Asking one thoughtful question.

Making one meaningful connection.

Standing in the group photo instead of slipping out early.

Visibility rebuilds gradually.

Confidence follows consistency.

Moving from title to identity.

Losing a title can unsettle identity more than losing income.

Without an employer's structure reinforcing a role, deeper questions surface.

Who am I without this position?
What do I offer beyond a job description?

So before walking into upcoming networking rooms, some questions have to be answered.

Without the former title, what remains?

Someone who works hard.

Someone people trust.

Someone who solves problems.

Someone who helps others move things forward.

Those qualities were never owned by an organization. They showed up in every role you held.

And they did not disappear when the role ended.

They are still yours.

A job gives you experience. But the judgment, resilience, and perspective you built over the years go with you wherever you go.

When employment changes, your name may disappear from someone else's organizational chart. But your leadership does not disappear.

In this season, you are the leader guiding what comes next in your life..

You decide where to show up.

You decide what to learn.

You decide who to reconnect with.

You decide how your professional story moves forward.

Rebuilding your network is not about proving you belong. It is about remembering that you do.

Show up to share. Show up to connect. Show up to listen.

Show up once more to practice being all of yourself again.

That is often where the path forward begins to take shape.

Sometimes it takes faith. Sometimes courage. Sometimes confidence you must borrow from your past until it feels real again.

And step by step, you walk forward.

"Prescence, not performance, is the long game of networking."

Chapter 8
You Were Never Meant To Walk This Alone

It all started with a mid morning phone call.

Not a strategy session. Not a business pitch.

Just a check-in between two professionals navigating job loss at the same time.

No agenda.
No performance.
Just honesty carried across a line that felt heavier than usual.

The fatigue was easy to hear. The uncertainty was familiar. The space between what had ended and what might come next felt wide and undefined. There was no need to talk about the tension. It could be heard in the pauses.

Both of us were standing in compounded loss—professional identity shaken, financial pressure, real grief layered quietly beneath responsibility.

So we did something simple.

We prayed. We kept connected and we leaned on each other. We made time.

At some point during that call, journaling was suggested. Not as therapy. Not as a polished exercise. Simply as a tool for clarity.

Capture the gap of what you have and need.

Name the swirl.

Write what feels unfinished.

Put language to what has been sitting unspoken.

Seeing thoughts on paper can steady them.

Then a question surfaced:

What if this season is not about our loss only?

What if this is a moment to change the narrative for others?

What if we wrote about this and encouraged other professionals to speak genuinely about job loss instead of fading into the shadows and whispering about it?

The ideas were not us being dramatic - just a desire to be productive in the waiting.

Purpose was needed.

A way forward was needed.

There was nothing glamorous about the motivation. It was grounded in responsibility and hope.

So we made a decision.

We would meet.

We would brainstorm.

We would collaborate on anything that might help us move forward and support our families.

Not someday.

Not when confidence fully returned.

NOW.

And we did.

We met and kept meeting. Some days were hopeful. Some days were tired. Some days unsure whether the ideas would grow or quietly disappear.

There were both moments of big energy and moments of big doubt.

But we kept showing up with laptops or even paper and pens.

Coffee shops.
Libraries.
Local picnic tables

Quiet corners wherever we could find them.

Free spaces, because money was tight and we were determined to keep moving forward.

Conversations that stretched longer than planned.

Progress did not happen in perfect conditions. It happened because we kept showing up.

The power was not in our brilliance.

It was partnership.

It was refusing isolation.

When one of us wavered, the other steadied. When one felt discouraged, the other offered perspective. Momentum did not come from perfection.

It came from consistency.

Healing is accelerated when we stop carrying the experience alone.

For us, deep and assured faith anchored the process. It steadied decisions and softened fear. Loss did not disqualify us.

It redirected us.

What first felt like interruption slowly revealed direction.

This book is the result of that decision to stay engaged instead of retreating.

You may not write a book.

You may not launch a project.

But you do not have to rebuild alone.

Reach out. Share honestly.

Invite someone into the process.

Progress moves differently when it is shared.

Isolation feels protective. Partnership builds strength.

Sometimes simply showing up together is the next right step.

And eventually something shifts.

It is not loud. No announcement marks it.

But you notice it. You are no longer only reacting to what happened.

You are choosing what happens next.

"Isolation feels protective, partnerships build strength."

Chapter 9 When the New Job Doesn't Quiet The Fear

If you are still searching for work, this chapter may feel premature.

Right now your focus may be simple: finding the next opportunity.

That is natural. Most people assume that once a new job arrives, the disruption of job loss will be behind them.

Often that is true.

But we want to share something we have heard repeatedly from colleagues who experienced job loss and later returned to work.

A quieter reality often follows the recovery.

The job returns.
The confidence takes longer.

Several professionals we know have said some version of the same thing:

"I thought getting a new job would fix everything."

Instead, something inside still felt unsettled.

Not broken.
Just different.

People describe walking into the new role excited and grateful for the opportunity. They want to succeed. They want to contribute.

And yet a new layer of self-questioning sometimes appears that was not there before.

Instead of listing every feeling, a few examples capture what many people describe:

• Double-checking work more than they used to.
• Watching leadership changes or company signals more closely.
• Wondering if positive feedback is truly sincere.
• Quietly asking themselves, Can I do this job? *Could this happen again?*

These reactions often surprise people, especially experienced professionals who were once very steady in their roles.

Researchers have studied this type of response after disruption.

A Brief Note On Hyper-Vigilance

After a sudden loss or disruption, many people become more alert to risks in their environment.

Psychologists sometimes describe this reaction as **hyper-vigilance**.

It simply means the mind becomes more watchful after something unexpected happens. Instead of assuming stability, a person may begin scanning for signals that things could change again.

This response has been observed after many forms of disruption, including workplace loss. It is not a character flaw. It is the mind trying to protect itself while trust rebuilds over time. *(American Psychological Association, 2023)*

You do not need clinical language to recognize what is happening.

A layoff reminds a person that work is not always as predictable as they once believed.

That awareness does not disappear overnight.

The important thing to remember is this:

Awareness does not have to turn into fear.

For a lot of professionals, the first months in a new role are simply a period of recalibration.

Helping Your Confidence Settle in a New Role

If you find yourself second-guessing your work after job loss, a few simple habits can help confidence rebuild.

- Ask your manager early how they define success in your role.
- Schedule regular check-ins so feedback is clear instead of guessing.
- Keep a small record of projects or wins during your first month.
- Focus first on learning the people and culture around you.
- Build one or two trusted relationships at work.
- Confidence rarely returns all at once.
- It grows through steady work, honest feedback, and time.
- Give yourself space to settle again.

You are learning a new organization.

You are rebuilding trust with new leaders and teammates.

You are allowing your confidence to settle again. That process takes time.

Interestingly, some professionals also notice positive changes in themselves after job loss.

They become clearer about the kind of leadership they want to work under.

They pay closer attention to culture.

They value honesty and stability more than titles alone.

In that sense, the experience may leave you wiser, even if it was painful.

If you recognize yourself in any of this at some point, pause for a moment.

You are not the only one who has felt this way.

Many capable, experienced professionals have quietly walked through the same internal adjustment after job loss.

Confidence rebuilds through consistent work, healthy relationships, and patience with yourself.

Over time the new rhythm settles.

Trust grows again.

The steady professional you have always been begins to feel familiar.

The layoff may have changed your perspective. It did not erase your ability.

You are still capable. You are still experienced.

And you are still moving forward.

Sometimes walking forward simply means learning to trust yourself again.

"Sometimes walking forward simply means learning to trust your footing again."

Chapter 10
Walk Forward

If you have made it this far, you have walked through a difficult landscape with us.

Let's recap.

You have seen the shock that follows job loss.
The quiet mornings when everything feels uncertain.
The loads of follow up paperwork.
The gap between what companies provide and what employees actually need.
Questions about identity and worth that surface when a title disappears.

You have also seen something else.

Movement.

Not perfect movement.
Not confident movement every day.

But movement forward.

The truth is, there was no single aha moment when everything and the path suddenly became clear for us.

There was no day when confidence returned all at once.

Instead, there were small decisions.

Phone calls.
Conversations.
Journal pages.
Coffee meetings.
Quiet prayers.
Ideas spoke out loud before they even felt fully formed.

Some of those ideas grew.

Some quietly faded.

Something important was also happening underneath all of it.

We were walking forward.

Not back to the lives we had before.

Forward into something new.

Along the way we learned something that surprised us.

This journey was never only about securing another job.

It was about becoming whole again.

It was about discovering that identity cannot rest only on employment.

Titles may change.
Roles may shift.
Organizations may restructure.

But your value travels with you.

You have walked through shock.
Through uncertainty.
Through rooms that once felt unfamiliar.

And you are still here.

That matters.

Some readers will already have secured new roles.
Some will still be searching.
Some may be building something different than they once imagined.

Wherever you are today, something important has shifted.

You are no longer only reacting.

You are choosing.

That shift from reaction to intention is growth.

You have learned to steady yourself when everything feels unstable.

You have learned to think clearly when your thoughts are racing.

You have recognized that identity must rest somewhere deeper than employment.

You have also seen the power of connection.

If you carry faith, you may look back and see that nothing was wasted.

If resilience is your anchor, you may say the same thing in different words.

Either way, you are not the same person you were before this season.

And that is personal development.

As you move forward, continue to show up.
Build relationships before you urgently need them.

Interrupt the narrative that questions your belonging.

Ask for help sooner.

Offer help when you can.

If hardship ever layers itself again remember this:

You have walked through disruption before.

You know how to steady yourself.

You know how to take the next step when everything feels uncertain.

You are not fragile. You are strengthened.

So wherever this book finds you today, we leave you with the same encouragement that carried us forward.

Keep walking.

May not be perfectly. One conversation.

One opportunity.

Faith was our anchor.

One courageous step at a time.

Walk forward.

"Keep walking - not perfectly, not fearlessly, but faithfully."

Closing Remarks

Before we close, we wanted to reiterate that we wrote this book honestly.

We did not write as experts standing outside the experience, but as professionals who walked through it ourselves.

We wrote while navigating uncertainty, asking hard questions, praying, journaling, meeting in borrowed spaces, and searching for a way forward that honored our responsibilities and our faith.

Some days we felt steady. Some days we did not.

But we kept showing up.

That is what this book ultimately represents.

Two people choosing not to carry loss alone.

Two people deciding that silence around employee job loss was no longer helpful.

Two people learning that courage does not always feel strong—sometimes it simply means continuing to move.

If this book found you during a difficult season, we hope it reminded you of something important:

You are not alone in this journey.

Loss may interrupt your path, but it does not erase your value.

Titles may change. Organizations may shift. **Your experience, character, and ability to contribute travel with you.**

Before closing this book, take a moment for yourself.

Pause and reflect:

What part of this journey felt most familiar to you?

What truth in these pages steadied you?

What next step feels possible now?

Write it down.

Say it out loud.

Share it with someone you trust.

And then take that step.

We are grateful you walked through these pages with us. Keep going.

Walk forward.

This book was written from lived experience—from seasons of uncertainty, rebuilding, reflection, and faith. Every insight, story, and belief shared throughout these pages is rooted in the personal journeys of the co-authors.

Artificial intelligence was used as an editorial and organizational tool in the preparation of this manuscript. It assisted with structure, refinement, and clarity. However, the heart of this book—its voice, convictions, and lived realities—belongs entirely to the authors.

Our hope is that what was shaped through our experience will serve as encouragement and guidance for yours.

Contributing Writer

My Walk Forward Was Building Something of My Own

By Danette Duron-Willner, Founder, Clearheaded, LLC and Employment Law Attorney

For more than two decades, I allowed part of my identity to be defined by the corporations that employed me. Part of the unspoken agreement to stay on that path often meant accepting and navigating being "the only" minority woman in the room.

That experience was not new to me. I was the only Latina in my elementary school, and later, the only Latina in my law school class. Over time, those experiences shaped how I showed up. Speaking up was rarely simple. It required calculation. When to speak, how to say it, and how to ensure it would be received.

A lack of representation created very little room for error. I learned to build my own sense of agency, but it came at a cost. Every word had to be intentional, structured, and clearly articulated in order to be heard.

That constant awareness of space, tone, and perception was exhausting.

And over time, that exhaustion compounded. A global pandemic. Ongoing corporate cuts. Downsizing, reductions in force, or what I once heard described as “management simplification.”

I remember that phrase clearly.

One morning, I walked into the office, greeted my VP, and by 10 a.m., I was seated in front of the CHRO being told that, due to management simplification efforts, an entire level of the organization had been eliminated. The VP I reported to was gone, and I would be expected to step in and lead the team moving forward.

That moment stayed with me.

In my 25 year career, I witnessed multiple reductions in force. I was often the one asked to remain. To stabilize teams, to manage the emotional impact, and to carry the work forward.

Until one day, I became the one impacted.

What surfaced in the aftermath was not just job loss. It was a burnout that I had been carrying for years without fully acknowledging it. My health had taken a toll. My marriage had ended. I found myself sitting in a post surgery appointment with my cardiologist, having a conversation about changes that could no longer be delayed.

I felt like I had hitI had rock-bottom.

And if I am honest, there was not a single moment where everything suddenly made sense. There were just small decisions. Taking time to rest. Paying attention to what my body was telling me. Allowing myself to consider that the way I had been living and working was no longer sustainable.

My resilience did not start in that moment. It had been built over time. Through personal hardship, through instability early in life, and through years of navigating environments where expectations were high and support was limited.

I also came to recognize the role of people. Mentors who invested in me. Friends and colleagues who reminded me of my value outside of a title. A chosen community that gave and received support in ways that were real.

I am now building my next chapter in entrepreneurship. I did not have everything figured out when I started. I began by taking what I already knew, my experience and my skills, and offering it in small, manageable ways. One conversation, one opportunity, one client at a time.

I created a business grounded in the expertise I developed over the course of my career, offering support to small businesses and nonprofit organizations in ways that are both practical and accessible.

Building and running Clearheaded LLC has given me the opportunity to partner with organizations that reflect both my experience, and my values

In many ways, I took the very experiences that contributed to my burnout and reshaped them into something more aligned with who I am now.

This work allows me to support organizations led by historically underrepresented founders. People who are building, often without the same access or support.

If I could say something to my earlier self, it would be this. You were never meant to stay small. The challenges you faced were not without purpose. They were building something in you, even when it did not feel that way.

For me, moving forward required a shift. I reached a point where I was no longer willing to carry the expectations and voices that had shaped earlier versions of myself.

The question became, if I am no longer defined by where I have been, what defines me now?

What defines me now is a commitment to honoring the journey, acknowledging the weight of it, and using those experiences to build something that serves others.

And if there is anything I have learned, it is this. Even when the path changes in ways you did not choose, you still have the ability to decide what comes next.

Tools

Appendix A
An Invitation

This book was written from lived experience.

We did not observe this journey from a distance—we walked it.

The idea to collaborate on this book was born while we were still unemployed, still healing, still trying to make sense of what had happened.

We began writing in the middle of uncertainty—navigating trauma, financial recalibration, and even moments of mental fog. These pages were shaped while we were still becoming.

This book was written for anyone who has experienced job loss—across industries, backgrounds, and faith traditions.

Yet, we would be remiss if we did not share what sustained us.

We did not come with extraordinary safety nets or abundant resources. What carried us was our faith in Jesus Christ. That faith was not abstract—it was stabilizing.

Scripture reminds us:

"For God so loved the world that He gave His one and only Son, that whoever believes in Him shall not perish but have eternal life."
— John 3:16 (NIV)

And:

"If you declare with your mouth, 'Jesus is Lord,' and believe in your heart that God raised Him from the dead, you will be saved."
— Romans 10:9 (NIV)

Faith in Christ does not remove hardship. It does, however, anchor identity beyond titles and secure hope beyond circumstances.

We extend this invitation gently and sincerely: if you are searching, rebuilding, or simply curious, you can turn to Him. No perfect words are required. He already sees you. He already knows your story.

You are not your job.

You are not your loss.

You are not forgotten.

You are loved.

Scripture Reflection:

The following scripture became an anchor during this season:

Scripture Reflections:

"Can a woman forget her nursing child, or lack compassion for the child of her womb? Even if these forget, yet I will not forget you." —Isaiah 49:15 (CSB)

*"You are not forgotten,
you are loved."*

Appendix B
Practical Resources

This portion of the appendix is designed to provide practical guidance without stigma. If you need these resources, use them confidently.

Unemployment Benefits

State-by-State Unemployment Insurance (UI) Resources (U.S.)

Why This Appendix Matters

Losing a job after decades of steady work can feel disorienting and deeply personal. Many people will avoid or delay filing for unemployment benefits because the process feels intimidating, confusing, and shame-filled. Unfortunately, delays and missed weekly certifications often result in lost benefits.

This appendix is designed to remove friction. It provides practical and expert guidance, lived-experience wisdom, and a reliable starting point for filing unemployment insurance claims in every U.S. state and the District of Columbia.

Before You File: Practical Best Practices

- **File as soon as you are separated from employment.** Waiting can delay benefits or reduce the number of payable weeks.
- **File in the state where you worked,** not necessarily where you live. If you worked remotely or in multiple states, your state agency can guide you.
- **Treat weekly or bi-weekly certifications like a bill that must be paid.** Set a recurring calendar reminder and complete it the same day and time each week.
- **Create a simple Unemployment folder (digital or paper)** that includes:
    - Separation notice or layoff letter
    - Last paystub
    - Employer name, address, and dates of employment
    - Government ID and Social Security information
    - **Ask for help early.** A friend who has recently filed, a workforce center, library computer lab, or scheduled agency appointment can make a meaningful difference.

- **Do not hide in shame.** Job loss is not a personal failure. Unemployment insurance is a benefit you earned.
- **Watch for scams.** Only use official state websites. Be cautious of texts or emails requesting personal information.
- **Plan for taxes.** Unemployment benefits are generally taxable at the federal level, and voluntary withholding may be available.

State-By-State Unemployment Insurance Filing Websites

Tip: Always access these sites directly by typing the address into your browser or using a trusted bookmark.

Alabama – https://uiclaimantportal.labor.alabama.gov
Alaska – https://labor.alaska.gov
Arizona – https://des.az.gov
Arkansas – https://www.ezarc.adws.arkansas.gov
California – https://edd.ca.gov
Colorado – https://www.colorado.gov/employment
Connecticut – https://portal.ct.gov/dol?language=en_US
Delaware – https://uics.delawareworks.com
District of Columbia – https://does.dcnetworks.org
Florida – https://www.floridajobs.org/
Georgia – https://www.dol.state.ga.us

Hawaii – https://labor.hawaii.gov
Idaho – https://www.labor.idaho.gov/
Illinois – https://ides.illinois.gov
Indiana – https://www.in.gov/dol/
Iowa – https://www.iowaworkforcedevelopment.gov
Kansas – https://www.dol.ks.gov/
Kentucky – https://www.kewes.ky.gov
Louisiana – https://www.louisianaworks.net
Maine – https://reemployme.maine.gov
Maryland – https://beacon.labor.maryland.gov
Massachusetts – https://www.mass.gov/topics/unemployment
Michigan – https://miwam.unemployment.state.mi.us
Minnesota – https://www1.uimn.org
Mississippi – https://www.mdes.ms.gov
Missouri – https://uinteract.labor.mo.gov
Montana – https://uid.dli.mt.gov
Nebraska – https://neworks.nebraska.gov
Nevada – https://ui.nv.gov https://nui.nv.gov/CSS/_/
New Hampshire – https://www.unemploymentbenefits.nh.gov/
New Jersey – https://myunemployment.nj.gov
New Mexico – https://www.jobs.state.nm.us
New York – https://www.ny.gov/services/unemployment-0
North Carolina – https://des.nc.gov
North Dakota – https://www.jobsnd.com
Ohio – https://jfs.ohio.gov
Oklahoma – https://oklahoma.gov/oesc/individuals.html
Oregon – https://secure.emp.state.or.us
Pennsylvania – https://www.uc.pa.gov

Rhode Island – https://www.dlt.ri.gov
South Carolina – https://www.dew.sc.gov
South Dakota – https://dlr.sd.gov
Tennessee – https://www.tn.gov
Texas – https://twc.texas.gov
Utah – https://jobs.utah.gov
Vermont – https://labor.vermont.gov
Virginia – https://www.vec.virginia.gov
Washington – https://secure.esd.wa.gov
West Virginia – https://workforcewv.org
Wisconsin – https://dwd.wisconsin.gov
Wyoming – https://wyui.wyo.gov

A Gentle Reminder

This process is administrative, not moral. Filing for unemployment is not a reflection of your worth, your work ethic, or your future. Ask for help. Take it one step at a time. And remember — this is a chapter, not the whole story.

Healthcare Coverage After Job Loss

Losing employer-sponsored health insurance can feel overwhelming, especially when it happens unexpectedly. However, there are options available, and applications can be submitted at any time following a job loss.

HealthCare.gov serves as the primary federal portal for exploring healthcare coverage options, including Medicaid and Marketplace plans based on income. It allows individuals to assess eligibility and, when applicable, directs them to their state agency to complete the application.

This is the best starting point for a national overview. It helps you determine eligibility, compare coverage options, and access links to your state's Medicaid application.

Medicaid.gov – Find Help

Provides direct access to your state's Medicaid agency, where you can apply for coverage or receive additional guidance.

State-Specific Portals

Many states have their own application systems. For example, in Michigan, residents can apply through **MI Bridges**.

Local Assistance (Navigators)

HealthCare.gov offers a *"Find Local Help"* tool that connects individuals with free, certified professionals who can assist with applications and answer questions.

Before applying, it is helpful to gather the following:

- Social Security numbers for all applicants
- Estimated household income for the full calendar year
- Date of loss of employer-sponsored health insurance

Taking these steps may feel unfamiliar, but these resources exist to support you during times of transition. Accessing healthcare coverage is not just a necessity, it is an important part of stabilizing your household and moving forward with confidence.

Mental Health Support During Transition

We know that job loss is not only a financial disruption, it can also impact emotional and mental well-being. Feelings of anxiety, grief, shame, or uncertainty are common, especially during periods of instability.

Support is available.

Reaching out, whether for guidance, counseling, or simply someone to talk to, is not a sign of weakness. It is a step toward stability.

Faith-Based Counseling

- **American Association of Christian Counselors**
  A directory of Christian counselors who integrate faith into mental health support.
- Many local churches and ministries also offer counseling or referrals, often at reduced or no cost.

Sliding-Scale & Low-Cost Services

- **Open Path Psychotherapy Collective**
  Provides access to therapists offering sessions at reduced rates (typically $30–$70 per session).
- **National Alliance on Mental Illness**
  Offers free support groups, education programs, and local resources across the United States.

Counseling Directories

- **Psychology Today Therapist Finder**
  A widely used directory that allows you to search for licensed therapists by location, specialty, insurance, and cost.

- **TherapyDen**
  A modern directory focused on inclusive, accessible mental health care, including filters for affordability and identity-based support.

Crisis Support

If you or someone you know is in immediate emotional distress, support is available 24/7:

- **988 Suicide & Crisis Lifeline**
  Call or text **988** to connect with trained counselors.
- **Crisis Text Line**
  Text **HOME** to **741741** to reach a trained crisis counselor.

A Final Word

Seeking support, financial or emotional, is not a confession of failure. It is an act of stewardship.

Taking care of your mental and emotional well-being is just as important as securing your next opportunity. You do not have to carry this season alone.

*"Seeking support,
financial or emotional,
is not a confession of
failure. It is an act of
stewardship."*

Appendix C

Reflections for Difficult Seasons

When Shame, Fear, or Uncertainty Appear

Job loss does not only affect finances.
It touches dignity, identity, confidence, and peace of mind. During this season, emotions may appear that you did not expect.

Shame. Fear. Confusion. Exhaustion. Doubt.

This appendix is not meant to solve everything. It simply offers reflections and scripture that helped steady the journey.

You may read one section today and return to another later. Take what strengthens you and leave the rest for another day

Scripture Reflections:

"The Lord is my light and my salvation—whom should I fear? The Lord is the stronghold of my life—whom should I dread?

When evildoers came against me to devour my flesh, my foes and my enemies stumbled and fell.

Though an army deploys against me, my heart will not be afraid; though a war breaks out against me,I will still be confident."— Psalm 27:1-3 (CSB)

When Your Mind Feels Foggy

You worked for decades. You built credibility.

You built stability. You built a life.

And now what? Everything feels different.

You sit down to prepare for an interview, and your mind feels foggy. You try to recall specific projects, timelines, outcomes—and the details don't come as easily as they once did.

You think to yourself,

I lost my job... am I now losing my mind too?

No. You are not.

What you experienced was not "just" job loss.

It was a traumatic disruption.

When stability is pulled out from under you, your nervous system responds. Your brain shifts into protection mode. Memory can feel scattered. Concentration may waver. You may struggle to articulate things you once spoke about effortlessly.

This is not incompetence. This is impact.

Trauma affects more than your bank account. It touches your sleep, your focus, your confidence, and your sense of orientation.

Research in psychological science shows that trauma and prolonged stress can temporarily affect working memory and other cognitive functions. When the brain is under emotional strain, it may struggle to process, store, and recall information as clearly as it once did—particularly when the stressor is significant or ongoing (Comer, 2025).

Be gentle with yourself. Your mind is recovering from shock.

Scripture Reflections:

"You will keep the mind that is dependent on You in perfect peace, for it is trusting in You."
— Isaiah 26:3 (CSB)

When Basics Become Mountains

There was a time when health insurance felt like an invisible utility—something always there.

You never thought about it. It simply existed.

Now you're looking at COBRA costs that rival a mortgage payment.

Thousands of dollars per month for coverage you pray you won't need.

And you sit there calculating:

Is this wise? Is this possible? Is this sustainable?

Suddenly, basic necessities can feel like mountains. Health Insurance. Unemployment paperwork. Benefit applications.

Things that once seemed simple now require emotional strength and energy you may not have.

Scripture Reflections:.

"Youths may become faint and weary, and young men stumble and fall, but those who trust in the Lord will renew their strength; they will soar on wings like eagles; they will run and not become

weary, they will walk and not faint." — Isaiah 40:30-31 (CSB)

The Humbling Moment

For many professionals, applying for unemployment benefits or Medicaid can be one of the most humbling experiences of their lives.

You may have degrees. Certifications.

Titles. Leadership experience.

You never imagined standing in this line.
Filling out this form.

Answering these questions.

There can be a quiet voice that says,

This isn't who I am.

But let's be clear.

There is nothing to be ashamed about.

You paid into these systems for years.

Every paycheck.

Every tax deduction.

Every contribution.

These benefits were not created "for other people."

They were created for citizens—including you.

This is not charity. This is provision.

It is not weakness to receive what you helped sustain.

There is no shame in taking a deep breath and saying,

"This is where I am right now."

The same discipline that built your career is now building your resilience. Redefining your dignity.

It is wisdom. Tell God what you need, and allow Him to lead you with wisdom as you make these important decisions.

Scripture Reflections

"Casting all your cares on Him, because He cares about you." — I Peter 5:7 (CSB)

"Those who look to Him are radiant with joy; their faces will never be ashamed." — Psalm 34:5 (CSB)

A Final Reminder

If you find yourself returning to these pages, remember this:

You are not alone in what you are feeling.

Others have walked through seasons of uncertainty and found strength again.

One steady step at a time.

"Dignity is not lost when your income changes."

Sources

USAFacts. (2026, February 28). *How many people are laid off in the United States each month?* https://usafacts.org/answers/how-many-people-are-laid-off-each-month/country/united-states/
(American Psychological Association, 2023)

LinkedIn. (2016). *Global Recruiting Trends Report.*

Jobvite. (2023). *Job Seeker Nation Report.*

About the Author:

Juanita Moore

Juanita Moore is an HR professional, strategist, and trusted advisor with nearly 30 years of experience in human resources, including leadership roles supporting large, complex workforces. She has guided organizations and leaders through some of the most challenging workplace moments, including employee relations, leadership accountability, and organizational change.

Over the course of her career, she has stood on both sides of job loss—advising leaders through layoffs and personally navigating the impact of her own career disruption—giving her a rare and balanced perspective on the human side of work.

She is the founder of Broad Moore Consulting, LLC, where she partners with small businesses to strengthen leadership, navigate risk, and build healthier workplace cultures focused on People. Purpose. Performance. Juanita is also a Community Health Worker and a certified Mental Health First Aider, equipping her to approach career transitions and workplace challenges with both practical insight and emotional awareness.

Her work is grounded in clarity, compassion, and a deep faith in God that even in uncertain seasons, there is a way forward.

Juanita holds a bachelor's degree from the University of Michigan-Flint, a master's degree from Cornerstone University, PHR and SCP certifications. She enjoys perennial gardening, coffee meetups, live music, and dancing.

www.broadmooreconsulting.com

About the Author:

Nichole T. Thompson

Nichole T. Thompson brings a faith-centered, real-world perspective to navigating life after job loss, grounded in resilience, purpose, and hope. She is passionate about meeting people where they are and connecting with authenticity so others feel supported, encouraged, and reminded of God's presence during uncertain seasons.

She is a seasoned audit, compliance, and risk management leader with more than 15 years of experience across complex healthcare organizations. Nichole currently serves as a Senior Compliance and Audit Consultant for a health plan and previously led an audit team as Director of Internal Audit for a healthcare organization. In that role, she established an internal audit function, developed high-performing teams, and helped design enterprise-wide compliance training programs. Her experience spans Medicare, Medicaid, and the Health Insurance Marketplace, guiding organizations—and individuals—through complexity, change, and regulatory demands.

Nichole has led high-impact audits, regulatory investigations, and risk assessments that strengthen internal controls and reduce compliance risk. She is a trusted advisor to executive leadership, known for delivering insights that support sound decisions and sustainable, compliant operations. She holds certifications as a Certified Internal Auditor (CIA) and Certified Healthcare Compliance professional (CHC).

Her perspective is shaped by lived experience, having personally navigated career disruption and its emotional and practical impact. This season deepened her faith in Christ and strengthened her commitment to helping others move forward with clarity and confidence.

Nichole holds a Bachelor of Science in Information Systems Management from Wayne State University and an MBA from Walsh College. She is a devoted mother, daughter, and servant leader who supports youth ministry initiatives and underserved communities in the Metro Detroit area.

About the Contributing Author:

Danette Durón-Willner

Danette Durón-Willner is a mom to a successful college freshman, first-gen Latina and founder of an award winning business, Clearheaded LLC.

Danette knows firsthand the tenacity and resilience it takes to build a career and a business from the ground up. With over 25 years of experience as a lawyer specializing in workplace rules and regulations, she spent decades helping large corporations handle complicated legal issues and working for fair treatment for their employees. This background gave her a deep understanding of how to protect a company while making sure people are treated right.

Three years ago, Danette started Clearheaded LLC to bring that high-level expertise to small business owners. She specializes in helping people who are often overlooked by the traditional business world, giving them the tools they need to stay out of legal trouble and keep their companies running smoothly. Danette sees herself as a partner to anyone brave enough to start their own venture, offering the steady guidance and support needed to turn big dreams into lasting, stable businesses.

www.clearheadedllc.com

www.ingramcontent.com/pod-product-compliance
Lightning Source LLC
LaVergne TN
LVHW020649100826
845148LV00012B/2391

9798904171841